MW01094367

WORDS NOT BULLETS

Michael Becker

First Edition, March 2015

Cover Design: Nessa Arcamenel
Interior Formatting: Nessa Arcamenel and Travis Simmons
Interior Illustrations: Michael Becker
Cover Photo: Paul Petoskey

ISBN-10: 0692413138
ISBN-13: 978-0692413135

Published in the United States of America

Michael did the art work for this Police patch
with the help of Officer Giles Anderson.

Thanks to all my fellow officer's for their help
and Tim Rynearson for teaching me brotherly love.

Acknowledgement

I wish to express my sincere thanks to Darlene Donaldson who was very instrumental in making of this work become a reality. Her encouragement was the motivating drive for what I would hope, the readers will enjoy for years to come. She worked very hard helping me with the selection of poems and my artwork seen within. She made several suggestions, exchanged interesting ideas, thoughts and enhanced this project which you see today. She was able to locate the publisher for me and then set out on a mission to get my book published. She came into my life a couple years before the passing of my wife Sheila to lung cancer. I am very proud to call Darlene my colleague, but more than that, she is first and foremost one of my dearest friends.

She is a grandmother of two, and dedicated to her family and church. I just wanted to thank her for all the help given and taking the time from her busy life to make this book possible.

Table of Contents

3RD PRECINCT ~ Love

4TH PRECINCT ~ Life's Journey

5TH PRECINCT ~ Passing Moments

6TH PRECINCT ~ Thoughts & Feelings

7TH PRECINCT ~ Loss & Loneliness

8TH PRECINCT ~ Dreams

9TH PRECINCT ~ Words

10TH PRECINCT ~ Light Shadows

1ST PRECINCT

HEAVEN

The Care Taker

As I step out into the night,
I wonder what might come my way.
For you see I must stand as a light.
To guide the ones who have lost their way.

Through storm or calm, I must still stand,
never yielding to what might lead me astray.
The shiny shield you see upon my chest,
Is a symbol of honor to meet the test.

It was given by all of you;
I am your servant, this is true.
But sometimes, I need a word of encouragement;
And a "Job well done."

To rise the spirit of this humble one.
The law was written by God,
Handed down to man;
All we can do is what we can.

Angels

Angels have been around since the beginning of time.
There are Angels for all uses;
Angels of deliverance
passing on the word of God
Angels to hold back the spread of disease
or the advancement of war;
Angels that communicate with the human race,
Angels for guidance to all types of destinations;
Angels with answers,
Winged Angels and Angels that took human form.
Angels are one of God's gifts to all mankind,
But there is one Angel that stands above all the rest,
She is the blue-eyed angel, the one I love best.
When she speaks it's like music to my ears,
Bringing hope, joy, peace and love to my sick heart;
When touched by her, I feel the warmth
of healing flow from her hands.
She is such a gift to all mankind;
a wonderful gift to be admired;
made of truth, caring, strength, courage and wisdom--
she is all this and so much more,
my Angel from the stars above.

Written on a lonely Christmas day

Michael Becker

Heaven

The pathway to heaven is a rough road,
Cluttered with the junk of mankind.
One misplaced step, you're down for the count,
caught up on mankind's slippery slope,

That slippery slope to nowhere,
The slope to sure death;
Death, the one thing none of us can avoid.
Is it permanent? Can be,

If it weren't for the gift given.
So precious it makes even this life worth living.
Belief in a man, full of grace,
gives us the key.

The golden key to that heavenly gate
That opens the way to his wondrous estate, an
estate not made with human hands.
The Master loves us, isn't that grand?

Through his love, we are able to enter his promised land.
But only through accepting his son, and his love
can a piece of this land be given,
this wondrous land that we call heaven.

Hello

Hello--I am not
alone; Never alone.
I have you
Always at my side,
For no price
of my own,
But the heavy
price you paid
so long ago;
Battered,
bruised & bleeding,
You hung there,
I thought,
just for me.
Not so--
for all.

Michael Becker

Humble Abode

Through the doors of our humble abode,
pass many people, young and old.
Meeting them with open heart and mind,
we find the pleasure of sharing precious time.
The love we have been able to receive and give,
gives us hope of the eternal life to live.
God has been gracious to all of us, his children,
by letting us know what it is like to be brethren.
God loves you and so do we,
someday, through love, all will be free.

On The Other Side of Midnight

On the other side of midnight,
there shines a bright new day.
It shines oh so brightly for me.
For you see, my love,
I walked out that evening to do what must be done,
to protect and serve everyone, and it worked out fine.
I was able to save a mother and baby,
and start a new lifeline.
Driving through the park
at this peaceful time of the evening,
I look at the swings
And visualize my little girl playing,
her mother pushing her high,
and the wind blowing through her hair...
Someone heard glass break in an alley,
its dark, and casually, he moves along.
Then there is a flash of light,
I fall, a burning pain in my chest;
I can't see; my eyes close; my heart stops, and
I start the long rest...
Friends stop by and try cheering you up.
It doesn't work, but they don't know,
because you're made of that kind of stuff.
Then there is the spit and polish;
they hand you a folded flag, and taps are played.
There is not a dry eye in the place.
But remember dear, on the other side of midnight,
there shines a bright new day.
It shines oh, so brightly for me.
That's the time we'll be together once again,
to walk hand in hand through the bright sun-rays,
for you see my love,
on the other side of midnight,
was made for you and me.

Michael Becker

Snow Fence

Old and rickety; it stood so frail and bent,
looking as if almost broken,
wooden slats thinner
than that of the old apple crate, of so long ago.
Held together by wire,
thinner than that which holds the bails
in the field tightly, in the brisk autumn.
This old rickety structure looking to the west
in anticipation of the onslaught of cold wind
that brings the snow of winter,
as Jack Frost tries to steal our breath.
One more winter this fence must stand
as it has so many winters before, but it pays a price:
once in a while, one of the frail wooden slats breaks away,
and is lost to the harsh winter at once.
We, like that bent weathered old fence,
must stand together, held strong by our faith,
united in the bond of brotherhood.
There are hazardous winds that blow upon us constantly,
not unlike that which blows against the snow fence,
attempting to destroy us.
Like that wire, Christ is interwoven between us,
as a common thread bonding us together,
making us stronger than as one.
True strength comes in unity,
a common belief in our Father and his love for us.
The snow fence is only strong because of its number;
we are strong because of our unity.
Like that old snow fence that weathers out the cool winter storms,
we too can weather out the storms of life--
if we do not try it alone.

Skinny Dipping

Walking down to water's edge,
stripping off your clothes to stand in the chill of the night,
illuminated by the silver glow of the pale moonlight.
Slowly you put your toe in,
wondering if the water will be cold or just right,
just a sample, not yet ready to take the plunge.
You find it warm as bath water, calming;
you ready yourself for the great lunge.
Diving, you swim under water,
toward the center of the pond,
eyes wide open, seeing nothing at all but darkness,
feeling only the warmth cleansing your body and soul,
setting you free.
One might feel they have returned to the womb,
to that time of peace and tranquility
before all the pressures of the world began to collide with you,
driving you to that deep despair
that we all feel from just living.
It's a time for being alone;
to withdraw into oneself and reflect,
to become one with the universe for a brief moment,
only having to share with one's self.

Michael Becker

Oh you can let someone come along with you,
on this special journey,
but it has to be someone very special
that you trust as much as you trust yourself.
You are naked, vulnerable and completely defenseless,
as if you were a grain of sand on a pane of glass,
where just the slightest breeze could blow you away,
never more to be.
It seems so simple,
just go skinny-dipping;
not so,
it's an experience as awakening
as standing naked before God.

*Dedicated to all the special people we find trustworthy enough
to love in the short time we have on this beguiling earth.*

The Glass Top Coffee Table

As I see it, religion is like a mirrored glass top coffee table,
So brilliantly bright, it's almost impossible to look at.
At the center under the table stands Christ our Savior,
Around the edge stand his twelve disciples.
Together they hold God up high,
For all mankind to worship.
Christ as was God's plan, was taken away from us.
Then, one by one, his beloved disciples fell by the wayside,
Until the table fell upon the floor and shattered
into as many pieces as there are churches throughout the world,
Each piece representing a church
as bright and shiny by itself as the whole had once been.
Each church has a piece of God, but not the whole.
So they strive as hard as they can to understand.
So they can reach the Promised Land.
We, as mortal man, look at all the churches around us
and become bewildered with the complexity of it all.
But there is hope! God would never let any of us down.
Christ will return, it's His promise.
And oh, when he does,
What wonders there will be to behold.
First, he will gather all the fractured pieces
of the mirrored tabletop back up,
And the face of God will be, once again, whole for all to see.
All those wonderful little churches will now be the whole
true face of God.
Because they kept their faith as best they could,
by always seeking the truth.
How we believe is not the question
it's how we got to that belief that matters, and that we believe.
Religion is not the question.
Christianity is the answer.

Michael Becker

The Pathway to Happiness

Happiness, they say, is just around the corner,
but there always seems to be just one more bend.
One more twisted turn, in the never ending pathway,
of uncertainty in life.

Happiness, like destiny, is in your own hands.
It's placed there, because it's part of the Master's plan.

Happiness is learning to walk through a river of fire,
With only a smile to protect you, like an asbestos suit,
from the intense heat.

Happiness, is a matter of choice; your choice.

The Master offers it, but you have to take hold of it,
then carry it,
it's a heavy load,
but well worth every ounce.

Happiness may be part of the Master's plan.
But no one ever said;
The pathway to happiness would be an easy one.

14

When one thinks of an Angel

To look into your liquid eyes
And feel the kindness reflected therein.

To feel the strength in your hand holding mine
Is to feel the courage locked in your soul;

To feel the heat in your body
Is to feel the passion in your heart.

To hear the honesty in your words
Is to know mankind has worth still.

To smell the aroma of you
Makes every breath I take a pleasure.

To have you let me share your space
Makes my walk through life of great value.

To know I will see you in the beyond
Will make my passing something to look forward to.

To simply think of all these things
Is to know I have walked with an angel.

Michael Becker

Thanksgiving Angel

A time of loving; a time of sharing;
Looking to the future; remembering the past.
Loving those with special caring for all;
Walking with a blue-eyed angel;
Holding memories in one's hand and heart;
To be shared with all before we part.
Even though we are now miles apart,
You gave me a stone as clear as glass,
Inside was my angel, oh so pure,
to carry with me through thick and thin;
filled with strength and love, deep within,
When alone and down-hearted
My angels love has started
to bring me back from the land of the departed.
Pure angel of love,
I thank you for sharing all your tools;
tools that help me walk through confusion,
One day I am up; one day I am down,
But never alone when you're around.
The clear Angel stone filling me with the warmth of your love;
All from my Thanksgiving Angel, sent from above.

Dedicated
To my Angel

Valley of the Sun

In the valley of the sun,
Life is always so much fun;
the sun never sets,
because the people keep the darkest of nights
Oh so bright from the heavenly light
That comes from each and everyone's love and joy
which spreads more than just light that guides us
It gives us the delectable delights
That make each and every one of us who we are,
So when we are down and our health is poor,
We receive the love and light to raise us up
so that we may stand tall and walk with the giants
That occupy the Valley of the Sun;
Giants made of kindness, caring and understanding,
But most of all love for one another,
So we say God bless one and all
THIS IS OUR HOME
The Valley of the Sun

*Dedicated to all the desperados
even the fastest gun in the
Valley of the Sun*

Michael Becker

2ND PRECINCT

FAMILY & FRIENDS

Children

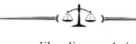

Children are like diamonds in the rough
That we must cut and polish
to make ever so tough,

so they might shine with an inner light,
to guide the ones that flow
through the troubled night.

Let's hope they choose the path that's right.

Friendship

Like love, there are no rules for friendship.
We can't force friendship,
any more than we can force love.
However rare love is,
true friendship is rarer.

To preserve a friendship,
three things are required.
To honor his or her presence,
Praise them in their absence,
And assist him or her in all their necessities.

Why do we live,
if not to make life less difficult for others?
True happiness doesn't merely consist
in how many friends we can count on one hand,
but in our choice and their worth.

Michael Becker

Grandfather's Prayer

To Cole

As I look down upon your pink little face.
I find myself asking God
to hold you in His amazing grace.

Pleading, Lord give me the knowledge to care for you,
then the strength to lift you up high,
and carry through.

Thank you for the musical patter of your little feet.
Your laughter, the smile upon your face,
makes you quite unique.

I love you and pray all things
that can cripple you stay away,
So that you can grow strong
and possess the gifts to save the day.

Morals that are strong, forged from his blood,
shed so long ago.
Will keep you far above the rest,
and always in the know.

As much as I love you, God even loves you more.
So I ask that He keep you strong,
as you pass through each door.

My Darling Sheila

My darling I love you. For you have done such tremendous things for me.

Darling, you are there when all else fails, my very fortress, where I can enter, when those that would harm me nip at my heels. No one can follow me in there and do me harm.

For someone so soft and tender, you are as rugged as the jagged mountains of the far west, holding back the assaults of all my enemies, as if I were safe in a tower of the castles of old England. If I were a knight of old, you would be my shield. Not even needing to be asked you are always there.

You have the ability to reach into my heart and still the deep, troubled waters that I find myself in from time to time, with just the soft whisper from your tender lips. All that bothers me becomes like clay in your hands, to be shaped and molded to your design.

On days when I am at my weakest, you hold me close to your breast, keeping me safe, giving me the time to regroup and once again become strong, so I can face the day.

Held in the embrace of your love, I find myself cloaked in the purity of your grace and spirit. You are all that makes me feel alive and complete.

Darling, you are not merely merciful, but mercy itself, taking away the pain; making me feel like I am in control; proud but humble at the same time.

My love, you give me the strength necessary for me to go wherever I wish. You give me the surefootedness, enabling me to walk the treacherous paths of life; Enabling me to reach the top of the mountain.

Your gentle ways have made me all that I am, or ever will be. Your golden word has made my own word straight and true.

The depth of your love reaches beyond heaven or hell. It is an inspiration, and without that very love, life on this earth would truly be unbearable.

Love, Michael

Michael Becker

My friend Bill

Walls of antique white,
Floors of stormy gray,
where I sat in deep thought
as the clock on the wall
Slowly passes time away.

This place is so full of sadness, and though
laughter's heard all around,
There's no gladness to be found.
People in sterile white
scurry around day and night.

My friend lies in bed,
Unable to speak or move.
With visions of greatness
that only dance in his head.

Eyes filled with tears,
his wife sets alone,
as if she were made of stone,
silently reminiscing over past years.

Will he once again rise?
Will he once again walk?
Will he once again think?
Will he once again talk?

Only God has the answer;
knows the end to the plot.
through him we can be great,
Whether whole or not.

Jack

I once had a friend named Jack.
Who lived his life as if he were a little laid-back.
But to everyone's surprise this was not true.
He believed in everything, right down to the red, white and blue.

He lived his life for others, full of love deep within.
A love so deep, some might think it came close to sin.
The first time I saw him, he was looking a little blue.
Buzzing down the street on his Amigo,
sitting there, as if stuck by glue.

On went the overheads, the siren did blare.
What a treat pulling him over, did we draw a stare,
Hey buddy, you got a license for that thing, out here on the run?
"I don't think so, officer," was his reply,
"Do I have to have a little fun?"
"No, my friend, you don't, but I just couldn't pass you by.
You looked so neat going down the road, I had to stop and say hi."

A friendship was formed, out of the best stop I ever made.
It developed, as we talked in the hot noonday sun,
with very little shade.
For the next five years, not a week went by
where we didn't meet because of my job, on the sly.
As I observed him, I found he always gave of what he had.
Always trying to set an example for his wife,
but most of all his sterling young lad.

Michael Becker

It worked out of this I am sure, for both his wife and his son.
They live their lives for others, never afraid of being under the gun.
They both do what is right, no matter what the price.
Jack would be proud of both his son and his wife.

He performed as if one of the greatest actors on stage.
I feel now as if I were his understudy,
and now that he is gone I hope I can do him proud.
A promise he never broke, of this I am certain.
Because he was full of love
until they brought down the final curtain.

I, as many others, wish from selfishness he were still here.
But he has gone ahead to prepare a better place,
for those he held so dear.

Looking down at him, I saw he was dressed the same as I,
when asked for help, put him to rest.
The same right down to his very vest,
somehow I knew I had passed the test.
God love him, my friend with M.S.,
who now runs his race with the very best.

Thank you Jack, for being my friend, setting the example,
for one to survive this dreaded illness,
but most of all, for teaching me to never stop loving
those that mean so much.

My Little Sweetheart

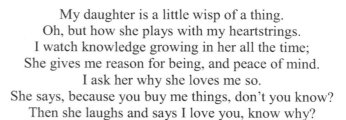

My daughter is a little wisp of a thing.
Oh, but how she plays with my heartstrings.
I watch knowledge growing in her all the time;
She gives me reason for being, and peace of mind.
I ask her why she loves me so.
She says, because you buy me things, don't you know?
Then she laughs and says I love you, know why?
Just because your my daddy, that's why.

Michael Becker

Small Way

I wake in the morning
to a bright new day;
I wonder what I might do
for a child in some small way.

Children are so small,
kind, loving and defenseless.
Dealing with problems
that even to us grownups seem offensive.

Most walk without the aid
of those who should care.
Going through life as if with blinders on,
unable to see the path,
But yet we grownups in our infamous wisdom
expect to hear them laugh.

Children; how precious,
the delicate little flowers of life,
Must be nurtured and cared for,
so they might learn to deal with its strife.

TOMBOY

The young lady that lives down the street
I find is quite pretty, but more than that, rather unique.
Most impressive is, she has a word like a man,
honest, solid and true, that you can bet will stand.
Looking like a boy, in her black tee shirt,
white shorts and baseball cap,
while she sits upon her tractor,
around her yard she makes her laps.
You wonder how, when she works
so hard both day and night,
One could remain so sweet, kind,
treating everyone with respect
and always so polite.
She walks erect, proud, and tall,
but most of all, so full of grace.
I am sure her mother and father
are proud this young lady doesn't just fill space.
It's a wonder at her young age,
how it is, she's so prim and proper.
When she is out with her friends and having fun,
I bet she is a real show stopper.
So impressed am I,
how at one moment, she can be a little tomboy,
the next a young lady at her very best.
The young man that finds this jewel
among the mud splattered rocks of today,
would be smart, to grab her up and make his nest.
I am so glad she lives down the street from me,
she is so kind, sweet, and full of love,
she reconfirms my faith in the young.
I know if I were in trouble,
she would be there, like an angel sent from above.

Inspired by Rhonda
Our next door neighbor.

Michael Becker

Young Lady

When you think of the words YOUNG LADY.
A beautiful picture is conjured up before your eyes--
Or it is before my eyes?
That picture is that of you.
You are the true essence of the words' very meaning,
Someone filled with dignity and poise.
Always willing to share of your plenty;
Your beauty is not just external--
But comes from deep within your eternal spirit.
You are so womanly, for someone so young.
I could sit and listen to the words you speak for hours.
When you open your mouth, you don't just make noise.
No, the wisdom that comes across your vocal cords
it's like music from the angels' choir way up high.
Friendliness is something not many possess, let alone share.
But for you to hold friendliness in, I am sure,
would fill you with great despair.
What I truly love about you is your unyielding honesty.
The way you can talk to someone about anything
that is of value in their life, at that moment.
Though things you have heard, I'm sure must have hurt,
through the portholes of your soul, no one would ever know.
No your eyes would just reveal peace, love, and deep, deep concern,
because you care so much, for all living things.
What a wonderful addition you are,
to this chaotic world we live in.

Inspired by Shelly
One of the kindest creatures
on this earth.

3RD PRECINCT

LOVE

Always

I wish you were here, my love;
I wish your heart was up close.
My love, those are the times that
I'm wishing the most.

I gave you my heart
To hold in your hand
Like time in an hourglass,
you let it slip away like sand.

I want you so badly, to hold
And to touch,
That is, my love, because
I love you so much.

And my dear, I want you to know
that whatever you do,
I will always be here,
No matter what, I will always love you.

Beginnings

Yesterday, I lay with my lover
and best friend, on silken sheets,
Our bodies entwined together
in our heated passion.
We laughed as we played with each other,
lost in the wonderful moment.
Together, we walked barefoot
along the beaches of life,
searching for sand dollars.
We frolicked in the sun and waves,
smiling like children.
We shared champagne and strawberries
as we rested on a towel
watching as the sun set in the west.
Last night, my lover,
best friend and I danced by firelight.
We swayed to the rhythms of the music
beating in our hearts.
Until, the cool night swept us up
in her embrace.
Today, I lay my lover and best friend
in the silken ground.
I watched silently
as she was swallowed by the dark earth.
I stayed behind with her
as they lay the sod on top of her,
lost in the moment.
Alone and crying,
I left a rose, strawberries and sand dollars
we had gathered along the way.
Now, I lie in my empty bed,
aching for my love.
Tomorrow, they would have laid me down beside her,
Had it not been for new love and new beginnings found.

Michael Becker

Christmas Wish

If I could have just one Christmas wish,
I would wish to wake up
every day,
To the sound of your breath
upon my neck,
The warmth of your lips
upon my cheek,
The touch of your fingers
upon my skin,
And the feel of your heart
beating as one with mine,
knowing that I could never find
that feeling
with anyone other than you.

Deep and Sensual

Deep and sensual
is the effect you have on me.
Making pleasure visual,
You help me see.

You slowly bring pleasure,
and fascinate my curiosity.
You bring me to heaven's gate
with your intimacy.

Taking me in your arms,
you soothe away my pain,
for which I am eternally grateful,
as you help me live once again.

You teach me to be free,
Look, my love, into my eyes;
Together swimming in our sea,
We slowly fall and rise.

Please sweetly kiss my lips,
gently part your way inside.
Together nothing we will miss,
from one another, nothing we will hide.

I will wrap you up in bedsheets,
keeping you safe and warm.
Feeling each others heartbeat.
as one till early morn.

You and I belong to eternal bliss,
we'll love again and then some more.
It all started with a kiss;
then forever my love, we will soar.

Michael Becker

Eternal Love

Do you love me, or do you not?

You told me once, but I forgot.

So tell me now and tell me true,

So all love can come flowing back to you.

Of all the people in this world I've ever met,

You are the only one I can't forget.

And if I succumb before you do,

In a lofty palace, I will wait for you.

And if you are not there by Judgment Day,

I'll know you slipped and went the other way.

I'll give the angels back all the heavenly things,

And risk the loss of all I have gained.

To prove my love is honest and true,

I'll go to fiery pits to retrieve you.

I Love Her

I love her in the morning,

I love her at night.

I love her when she is wrong,

I love her when she is right.

I love her when she hurts me;

I love her when pleasure she offers.

I love when words she uses sound like hell;

I love her, with all her imperfections;

I love her, with all her strengths.

I love her--just because I love her.

Michael Becker

Life Time Partner

When you ask her to be one with you
Are you a man of your word?
True to yourself
most of all, are you a liar?
Be honest....
Is her beauty all you see?
Even if, in the eyes of the world,
she is not very pretty.
In honesty, is she everything you wish her to be?
If not, stop!
Don't lose all you ever will be.
If you step to that altar
Giving your word to her and God,
It better be true.
Or you have lost all you ever will be.
But if in your mind's eye
You see all you'll ever want
Praise the Lord, full speed ahead;
You will have nothing to dread,
You will stand heads above the rest,
Passing with ease all the test
You two will be as one, the very best.

Heart & Head

With beauty and without warning,
you walked into my life.
Looking at her you could see, without a doubt,
her life was full of strife.

As I would sit and listen to her life,
present and past.
I could not but wonder,
how this delicate little creature could ever last.

Looking deeper I observed
how she took everything in that was around.
Took it in, no matter how nasty or bad,
making something of beauty from it,
giving her an anchor to this fertile ground.

How lucky I was, to be able for a brief moment
to come together with her for sharing.
She was filled with so much love, friendship, understanding,
and great depth for caring.

In the security of my mind's eye, I took hold of her
and we started off down the road, hand in hand.
Where we transcended, as if on Aladdin's carpet,
to some far magical, mystic, distant land.

Michael Becker

Coming together, lying in the soft grass,
surrounded by wild flowers of multi colors, in a fertile field.
Bodies gently touching, we felt warmth rush through,
the warmth only love can make one feel.

Lying my head gently upon her firm, but soft breast.
I felt so safe, complete, and at total peace and rest.

Picking up a rose, gently I caressed the soft scented petals
across her slightly parted lips.
Gently cradling her in my arms,
I kissed her closed eye lids.

Slipping back into reality, I quietly closed the coffin's lid.
For you see, the love I feel for her, is never to be shared.
I'm just so lucky, that she even looked my way or even cared.

She is so wonderful, kind and caring, way out ahead.
She could be loved in my heart and my head.

Love

Love is not just a word or a single action.
Love can never lead you astray; it's pure truth.
Like God's perfect morning, in the sunrise,
it is filled with warmth.
Love is many hidden things, yet it exists--
sometimes in the smallest places in the heart--
But once found, it can bloom.
Fear can make it choke in your throat;
Joy can bring you to tears.
Love, unlike things of evil,
Never hides in the shadows or the dark.
Love never feeds on deception.
You think it ignores you,
Then, there it is, where you least expect it,
when you have given up all hope,
growing with the fertilizer--
Trust, honesty, and compassion;
Nothing less, and much more.
When you think you found it,
It will turn you down cold.
When you think you have escaped it;
You will find love has you in its hold.

Michael Becker

Love's Demise

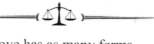

Love has as many forms
as there are colors and fragrances
in the garden of life.

If it weren't for the many
colors and fragrances of love,
the beauty of the garden,
would be lost forever, to the world.

And for all those who would take the time
and have the courage,
to reach in and gently caress
the soft petals of love.

But one must remember,
to leave love as they found it,
unmolested,
as they would want the flowers of the garden,
to be left
unmolested.

Love is meant for the enjoyment of all
who are fortunate to be blessed with the opportunity
to have been caressed by its warm touch,

Never for those who would reach in and pluck it
from the garden of life,

to let it wither and die, on the cold ground, never to
be enjoyed by anyone,

Causing love's demise.

My Heart Belongs to You

As I set and ponder
over the delights of your fruits,
I feel my inner self come alive.
I am filled with the very essence
of your flowing energy.
It is as if my very soul is set afire.
I am so hot from your heavenly glow,
as if I were in the very fires of hell,
where only your undying love could carry me through.
When I enter your space, I know I am at your very core,
the center of what I hope is now my universe,
then you reach out with your sweet, loving heart,
letting me know we will never part.
You hold my heart in the palm of your hand,
and whisper softly, making me understand
that I am a man worthwhile and true,
All because my heart now belongs to you.

Michael Becker

Ready For Love

Take my hand and lead the way;
please tell me all you have to say.
Whisper softly in my ear,
all those things I want to hear.
Kiss my lips and touch my skin;
bring out the passions hidden deep within.
Pull me close and hold me near;
take away my pain and fear.
In the darkness of the night,
be my beacon, shine your light.
In the brightness of the sun,
show me that you are the one.
Give me wings so I can fly,
for I can soar when you're nearby.
Enter my heart, break down the wall,
it's time for me to watch it fall.
I've been a prisoner, can't you see?
Break my chains and set me free.
Strip me of my armor tight,
you'll find I won't put up much of a fight.
Release my soul held deep within,
I'm ready now, let love begin.

Secret Love

I would rather love you than make love to you.
As wonderful as I am sure it would be to make love to you,
it most probably would be just a fleeting moment,
to be cherished for certain, but just a moment,
no matter how warm and wonderful it might be,
to have your naked, goddess-like form lying next to me.
where we could move slowly together in perfect harmony,
hopefully giving each other pleasure,
a wonderful moment suspended in time.
To make love to you would be such a wonderful experience,
but if in the end I were to fail you, and you were to turn your head.
I would, without a doubt, surely feel as if I were dead.
No, I would rather love you deep within my heart,
because to love you deep within my heart is forever.
To love you, is to know wherever I am,
all I have to do is close my eyes and there you would be,
in my mind, to hold, talk to, to help, and appreciate.
I would never fail you, because love is unfailing,
it's real and forever.
Death can't even extinguish love.
To love you, you don't even have to be told,
it can be my secret, locked away deep within my heart;
it's simpler, that way no one can be hurt.
There might be pain, but that pain would be mine, never yours.
When one loves, it should never cause pain to the one they love.
So all I can say, though you will never hear,
is thank you for walking in my space
and filling it with the essence of your beauty--
and I don't mean just your physical beauty
of which there is plenty--
but the most important beauty,
that emanates from deep within you,
right down to your very soul.

Michael Becker

She

She is my life,
my soul,
my everything.

From morning to night,
she made everything right.

Giving all she had
and even more;

Never locking me out
or shutting the door.

The Rose

I had a rose sent to me today.

It came in a very special way.

This rose was made by the Master's hand.

I believe there is none better, throughout the land.

I always thought the black rose was the best,

But this beautiful pink rose beats all the rest.

The florist always wins, with the black rose in competition,

but they have never been in my heavenly position.

I think "Angel" is the name I'll give this rose.

Because an angel sent it, as everyone knows.

Thank you for the pink rose, my love.

A beautiful rose sent from above.

Michael Becker

What is Love

Love is when you are willing to give all you have,
expecting to receive nothing in return.
If you expect to receive when you give,
then you have given nothing at all.
If everyone was willing to give all the time,
the world would be filled with love,
and love is all that really matters.
Love is listening and understanding,
when everything logical tells you different.
Love believes, when there are no facts,
to support that believing.
Love is unselfish and all caring,
maybe one-way, but not usually.
Receiving one's love
without question is the very essence of love.
Honesty is the heart of love, its very core;
if it is not there, there can be no love.
Listening is all-important, for the growth of love.
Touching is as the suns warmth is to the earth,
giving energy to all those we love, so they might survive.
Believing in love is to believe in yourself.
Because if you don't believe and love yourself,
you can never love anyone.

You

I live for only one reason, and that reason is you,
to give myself to you is so important.

Loneliness hunted me at every step, until there was you,
you are everything: morning, noon and night.

Walking through life,
I never saw the things of beauty along the way,
then someone took me by the hand;
that someone was you.

There were fragrances all around me,
I never noticed,
then I stopped, bent to one knee,
and noticed them all,
because of you.

I never would have felt the gentleness
of a rose against my lips,
but I did and much more,;
what a gift I have in you.

To love God as I do, I am sure I would have,
but the closeness I feel to him could only be achieved
from my loving you.

Michael Becker

Your Beauty

God, you are beautiful beyond compare.
You might say, compared to what?
Well let's start with a sunset, as it plays its colors
across the soft bellies of the puffy clouds in the heavens above,
as the mysteries of night descend upon us.
The mysteries of you are always so exciting,
filling my life with electricity;
The power necessary to supply me with the energy
to keep up with and perform for you.
To hear your voice
is like being in the finest of concert halls of the world, where
the acoustics are in perfect harmony with nature.
Bringing the softest of music to caress my ears,
making me feel alive and filled with your essence.
You are so full of wisdom, and compassion,
So that whenever one is near you
they are filled with the liquid fire that flows
from deep within your soul.
When you walk across a room,
it's like everyone stops whatever they are doing
just to take in the gracefulness you fill that room with;
Gracefulness not unlike that of the gentle breeze,
that plays its way across a field of wildflowers,
butterflies float therein,
their wings reflecting a multitude of color
in the warm afternoon sun.
To love you is the easiest of all things on this earth to do.
Because of the essence of you: your beauty,
not only your outer beauty,
but most of all, your inner beauty,
which has no equal.

Your Loving Face

As I set, pondering over time and space,
one recurring memory keeps coming up.
The pleasant smile, the gentleness and love
I have always seen reflected upon your loving face.
Life has so much meaning when I am with you;
I know God has surely sent you.
When times are hard and my back is bent
from the weight of every day stress,
there you are,
to give me strength to stand tall,
meet and conquer whatever the test.
God loves me, I know, of this I am sure,
that's why he gave me you, whom I hold so dear,
So I might have just a little bit of heaven
while passing through this hell on earth.
Thank you for the good moments
that surpass and outweigh all the bad.
I only wish I could have done so much better
for you, given so much more.
I love you, my darling, and that's for sure,
for no mortal man unworthy as I,
could have ever expected to rise so high,
Except through the presence of God,
and what I have seen reflected in your loving face.

Michael Becker

4TH PRECINCT

LIFES JOURNEY

Alive

Did you ever, upon waking, look out at the world,
to find the fog so thick
that everything seemed damp and dreary?
Your very spirit seems to ebb and flow, slipping right away,
spinning your very soul on a downward spiral,
into a deep dark pit of depression.
Well, that feeling just doesn't exist for me,
because you, like the sun burning away the foggy mist,
coming through the window of my heart, warming my soul,
make me feel as fresh and clean as the damp heavy morning air,
filled with fragrances of a field full of wild cherry blossoms,
carried with the wind.
To see the impish smile upon your face
chases all the demons of depression away,
Rekindling the fire of my spirit,
giving me the essence needed to be a man.
When I look upon your face,
I can see that it has been kissed by the Gods,
caressed by the winds that gently blow
through the streets of heaven,
and cleansed by the gentle tears of the gods,
these tears we call rain.
Then you speak with wisdom,
compassion and tenderness,
and I know if tomorrow never comes,
at this moment I am full and complete,
Alive.

Blown Away

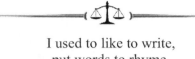

I used to like to write,
put words to rhyme,
making this earth we live on
more bearable; a little more understood.

But things change, become confused;
Words, meaningless; with little effect,
now flow from the end of my pen,
making scratching noises oh so thin.

Writing, why? What's the use?
Who enjoys it or even understands?
Oh there are those that say, what joy!
But in reality, they are just annoyed.

Life, sometimes, is like writing;
Seems meaningless, with little direction.
If anything at all, we're just here.
Like the seasons, spring, winter, summer and fall.

In the end, we will all disappear.
Like the paper written upon,
Gone, like the conclusion of a long day.
Crumpled, turning to dust--and then blown away.

Michael Becker

Old Man

I once saw an old man come down a crooked path,
winding through the woods,
where he came to a rest,
and began to spin a tale at his very best.

When he spoke, it was of things of long ago,
a time when the land was young,
the forest a virgin stand,
untouched by human hand;

Of a time when this man
put his ax in his blistered hand to work,
taking many whacks
at God's mighty piece of work.

Listening to him talk,
I couldn't help but take a look around;
what did I see but that the woods
were as thin as was he.

The woods stood crooked
and bent on this little piece of land;
as crooked and bent
as this old gray-haired man.

It made me wonder who had prevailed, man or forest.

One thing is for certain: when this little old man is gone,
the forest that once mighty stand,
will live on, no matter how blistered the hand.

*Inspired by the words spoken from a little old man
to his grandchildren.
In Heartwick Pines, Michigan State Park.
From his days as a lumberjack*

Another Day

Life can be so lonely and depressing,
without meaning or direction, if you let it.
Life can be all work, no play,
filled with pain, with no peace, if you let it.
Life is hard; you give all you have,
but it expects more, so much more, if you let it.
When I awake in the morning, it's like never having slept.
If you were to work beyond your endurance, a week with no rest,
you would just began to feel the pain I feel in this body of mine.
To just rise from a bed is like running a marathon,
but yet I have all my daily tasks ahead of me,
like bending to put my socks and shoes on,
buttoning my shirt or putting my legs into my pants.
Looking at the door to your bedroom,
you pray you can make through one more day.
One more day without falling, or looking foolish,
but most of all not embarrassing those around you,
especially the ones you love.
Then off you go to face the new day.
As hard as it is, it's all worth it you see--
when you reach the living room,
you get to look into the eyes of someone special,
and so full of life, ready to meet the new day and life's challenges,
without the slightest fears.

Michael Becker

That person has the ability to laugh at almost every adversity
they come up against.
My body might be wracked with pain,
but my mind is filled with pleasure,
contentment and inner strength just by her presence.
The doctors may have all the medicines on this earth
to make you feel good,
but they don't work.
Let me tell you,
the love I feel from that one special woman of mine
can't be bottled, or put in a pill or capsule.
She spreads warmth all through me
with just a kind word, touch or look.
She makes this meager life I live worth it all.
When I am with her,
the greatest athlete in the world comes in second place
next to me, that's the kind of strength she shares with me.
She makes me feel that I am someone of value,
worth having around,
giving me my reason to exist.

Born to Wander

She was born under a wandering star,
her heart forever to wander, but not too far.

She kept her heart under lock and key,
never knowing how to let it out; how to be free.
Letting the world see her in all her naked splendor,
as if baring her soul: little did they know.

Her beauty was beyond compare; soft eyes of liquid fire,
made you wish you were the only one they had ever burnt.
I had the pleasure of loving her; did she care?
Love was something she didn't know how to share.

She was born under a wandering star;
her heart forever to wander, but not too far.

There were those that hated her; some called her tramp,
some called her whore, some called her bitch.
Wishing she were dead, lost to the world,
finding her beautiful body in some cold water filled ditch.

Even though she was lost, making you feel the same,
how wonderful to have her pass by;
your heart would skip a beat.
How she made you wish you could fall upon your knees,
to worship at her feet

She was born under a wandering star,
her heart forever to wander, but not too far.

Michael Becker

Loving her was the easiest of all things,
but alas her trips into the night, knowing there purposes,
tore my heart out, almost tearing it apart.

When I watched her walk out the door each time,
over her face there seem to come a look of horror,
as if she were a lost child, melting into the landscape,
from which there was no escape.
A fear would spread over my body,
that the next time I would see her, it would be in her grave.

She was born under a wandering star,
her heart forever to wander, but not too far.

Yes, she was born under a wandering star,
and each and every night, before my head touches the pillow,
I pray she will go far.

I love her, and my home is always hers,
but I fear she will be lost forever
to the world she tried so hard to please.
She probably never knew
just how her mere presence lit up the world,
in simply being, she pleased all who came in contact with her.

There are those who would give all they had
to make love to her,
I would give all I have just to love her;
even more if she could feel real love, from anyone.

She was born under a wandering star,
her heart forever to wander, but not too far.

Broken Promises

A promise broken is a fortune lost,
one's assurance gone amuck.
Words, who would think,
Who would even know their real consequences?
But yet each and every one of us is judged
of our use of reckless words.
The shake of the hand; a man's word, used to be his bond--
not anymore.
Now, he or she just takes the spoils they can reap
and then turn and vanish out the door.
Loves are lost, countries set asunder,
just for the absence of trust, by the breaking of one's word.
Once a person breaks their word,
nothing else really matters: how can it?
From that moment on, whatever promises are made,
might as well be words cast into the wind.
Oh, the way we twist and deceive, mixing our words together;
making all we do wrong seem right.

Michael Becker

Free Spirit

As I sat on the patio
soaking in the warm rays of the sun.
I looked out at the brown chestnut
running free in the field.
Its tail out straight,
mane blowing in the breeze.
So graceful in its sprints and turns,
as if a belly dancer spinning in midair.
I thought of you.
You have a spirit
that strains on its tether to be free.
I could see your hair
like that wild mane blowing in the air,
as you ran through the fields bare as a new born.
The only difference
unlike the tether on the chestnut,
you have a self-imposed tether.
Keeping yourself in check.
Only because of the silly rules
society places upon you.
No, if you had your way, you would run free
and do anything in your heart,
as long as it hurt no one else.
Because as wild and free as your spirit is,
you have a gentle side.
A side that cares;
cares for the feelings of all those around you.
Your spirit is special--
Unlike any I have ever known.

Inspired by Amy
The freest spirit I know

If

If I were to stumble and fall,
could you still see me as that man,
you once saw standing tall.

If I were not able to smile
my wide usual smile,
would you smile for me?

If I were to cry out from pain,
would you be able to kiss my forehead
without turning away.

If I were to laugh a little weak,
would you still think
I was someone rather neat?

If I were to yell out from the pain,
would you be there
when I turned around?

If I fell asleep from exhaustion,
would you hold my hand,
until I once again could stand?

If I were to drop my dinner plate,
would that be the one thing
that would seal my fate?

Michael Becker

Made by the Master's Hand

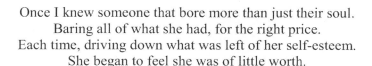

Once I knew someone that bore more than just their soul.
Baring all of what she had, for the right price.
Each time, driving down what was left of her self-esteem.
She began to feel she was of little worth.

But why not, her life had been completely scarred.
Right from the start, every man seemed to look
and think of her as just a piece of meat.
Adopted father, foster father, brothers,
men by chance she might meet.
She was taught quite young, how to survive out on the street.

Her beauty did not help; it just drew attention to her.
Hiding all her good qualities, of which there were plenty.
Even men, who professed their love,
had no idea she was sent from above.
Thinking she was cheap, calling herself a whore,
she felt all that she was went out the door.

Sometimes, I even wonder how she could have made it so far.
Will her life, when it's over, be completely marred?
But she must be in tune with the one up above,
for I have never met someone so full of love.

Now nudity might not be a bad thing in the right place,
it might bring inner peace.
She belongs on a canvas, as a work of art,
not on the lap of some old fart.

Her beauty could have only been created by the Master's hand.
Life can be happy, full, and fun; for her there is a lot at stake.
But as far as low esteem, forget it,
like I said, made by the Master's hand.
And the Master makes no mistakes.

Doors

I hit the road, out on the skids.
An old man, going nowhere fast.
Looking around, seeing nothing at all,
I am sure all I've missed will be my down fall.
Alone behind the wheel, I head down the road,
after hearing another door slam behind.

This has been going on for longer than I care to remember.
As a child, the voices I heard were hard and cruel,
cursing at each other,
as they slammed out the door, leaving me alone.
Out on the road throughout the day, and into the night,
only coming in because I was afraid of the dark.

As a young man, nothing much changed,
those I loved still spoke with hate;
I was still alone, afraid and out on the town rather late.
Going home was not for me;
As I saw it;
it was not in my best interest.
So off to the air force, a new road I did travel,
only to find harsh words spoken once more
forcing me out one more door.

Michael Becker

Your roots have a way of haunting you, drawing you back.
Although confusing, leaving you most times in the dark,
making you wonder 'Where's the spark.'
Harsh words again; Mom and Dad saying we are going to part,
slammed whatever door might be opening completely shut.

Now a man of full age, married, with daughter and son,
you would think life would be full, and you would be on the run.
But along comes so many illnesses
slamming shut yet another door;
leaving you a mess lying on the floor.

But yet through all this, I have been able, once in a while,
to give life a gentle kiss,
by helping someone along the way,
passing through each door.
And in the end, when I am bent and so thin,
maybe I won't mind so much passing through that last door,
that never slams shut.

Words not Bullets

Getting High

Some people get high on drugs,
others on booze, coffee, or on a million other things.
I got high on walking the razor's edge.
The high I had was as high as any high could get.
Fear, the thrill of victory, and paranoid feelings were the greatest.
To walk in any situation, dangerous or otherwise, was the best.
Getting up in the morning and pinning my badge on my shirt.
Was the same as sticking a needle in my arm,
loaded with heroin, cocaine, L. S. D.
and marijuana all at the same time.
I walked out the door high, ready to face the world
and any task that might lie before me.
But as with any high, there is only one way to go, down.
And in most cases there was no way back up.
When you think you are the best at what you do
is when you make the worst mistakes that can be made.
To try to stay humble, is impossible.
No matter what you do, how good it turns out
you probably did it for all the wrong reasons.
There are always those around you,
eagerly ready to polish your armor.

Michael Becker

So you can go out and dazzle all those around you,
friend or foe, with your brilliant reflection.
Key word: reflection.
What is a reflection, but the brightness of others
bouncing off of you, nothing of yourself.
When you look your best is probably when you are at your worst.
Being high has a price,
please, let me share what that price is with you.
As I see it, the price is too high,
and I am glad I no longer have to pay it.
The first payment is yourself.
The second payment is all that is important around you;
your loved ones, your home, I mean everything.
If you are lucky something comes along,
destroying whatever makes you high.
You walk away, not unhurt, but you walk away--
then you can deal with what really matters in your life.
You don't need to get high, no matter what the reason;
just deal with whatever comes along,
HONESTLY!!!!

Obligations of Man

To walk through life, as the fly might cross rice paper,
as gentle as the bee caresses the rose,
never causing a tear or disturbance.

Having a genius to reach into the garden of life
and rip out the weeds,
so that the flowers and fruits may reproduce in all their glory,
that life might go on.

To listen to the music of a butterfly,
dancing on multi colored wings,
lie in a field and watch the grass grow,
the breeze gently caressing its tips.

Loving all of God's creatures for what they are,
recognizing their purpose,
in the never-ending reason of things to be.

Michael Becker

Roots

I am as lonely as the old tree
standing at the center of a vast prairie.
Surrounded by tall golden grass
and a multitude of colorful flowers.
My branches are cracked and bent
from the many forces of nature.
They have battered this once-youthful sapling
into a ridged, brittle old tree,
with just the passing of time.
But, my soul, my very roots reach deep
into the bowels of Mother Earth.
If it were not for this connection,
I know I would surely fall over
with the slightest breeze and perish.
The time will come when
either by wind, water or fire,
this brittle tree will fall
and succumb to this place.
Then pass on to a place filled with love,
to once again stand tall and proud.
Limbs outstretched with love to embrace eternity,
never more to stand alone.

Self Portrait

You may not know it to look at him,
But he believes in mermaids and fairytales;

He believes in love at first glance,
And "happily ever after's";

He believes in the good in others
And in forgiving and even sometimes forgetting.

He dances in the rain,
And smiles at strangers;

He gives his heart completely,
And never asks for return;

He is a father, a son,
And a lover;

He is a friend
And a companion;

He is a passionate being,
He is a man;

But most of all,
He is me.

Michael Becker

The Dark Side of Life

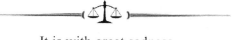

It is with great sadness,
I look into the well of life,
only to see the dark water moving
ever so slightly, if at all;
dropping a small pebble, causing a ripple to appear
upon its mysterious face,
only to see it smooth out once again,
as if it had never been disturbed.
Can the dark lonely waters ever sparkle and glitter,
like that of the mountain stream
cascading over the rocky terrain
on it's never ending journey
to a fertile green valley far below,
where it comes to rest in a clear, shimmering
emerald pond full of life.

Truth

Hello son, what is your name?
I have come here to help you.
Anything else would be a shame.
You see this badge upon my chest?
It's a badge of honor;
A challenge for me to meet the test.
To do for you and everyone
The very best that can be done.
This life is a lonely one to say the least.
But listen to my words.
Surely you'll find, I am no beast.
The sweat you see upon my face
Is really hundreds of tears.
That, for sure, is no disgrace.
They were shed for young people,
like you yourself,
That I have failed to help.
So, young man, give me your name,
for I'm sure by now,
You can see that this is no game.

*Dedicated to Steve for his help in
making me better understand
the youth of our fine city.*

Michael Becker

Warrior

I am a man with little learning,
But can be wise;
I am a man with little silver or gold,
But I am wealthy.
I am a man with peace in my heart,
But with a heart of a warrior.
I am a man that has been betrayed;
But I trust with all I am.
I am a man beaten,
But I stand victorious.
I am a man bruised and battered by the wind,
But not broken or tamed.
I am a man whose body is ill;
But I stand whole.
I am a man held down by all the world's weight
But still I am all powerful.
I am a man with hands tight upon my throat,
But I speak freely from the heart.
I am a man raped by the corruption of man
But I am true and pure;
I am a man with clipped wings,
But I take flight with the eagles.
I am a man whose heart has been ripped,
But it's stronger and larger than before
I am a man happy,
But able to cry;
I am a man full of fear,
But I stand alone, and unafraid.
I am a man strong and virile,
yet scared.
I am a man; just human,
But I am to some, almost divine.
I am a man; blood, bone, sexual.
But I am so much more
I am a man, a warrior;
But I hope much more.

The Ditch

There is a ditch that runs clear across America,
filled with some of most vile and corrupt things
ever put on this earth by man.
I don't just mean the waste left behind
from mankind himself;
What is left is grief, broken bodies and hearts, frail shells
void of the emotions necessary to sustain life.
Children are left fatherless or motherless,
whatever the case might be,
just discarded along the way,
in the ditch to fend for themselves;
Left like that old rusty pop can,
to cause agony and pain
to whomever they come in contact with.
In this ditch you can find lost souls, lost loves, lost courage;
there are so many things lost that are left behind on it.
How many times while traveling the ditch
have you seen the discarded waste along the shoulder,
I bet you have.

Michael Becker

If not, maybe it's time you took notice;
stop pick it up and cradle it in your arms for a while,
hoping it has not been battered and bruised beyond repair.
You know with kind words and gentle nurturing,
you might be able to stroke a battered, injured ego back to health;
giving someone the tools necessary to carry on.
By finding the right words to stroke the injured ego,
when there are so many reasons they have been broken,
and nearly, if not completely, destroyed.
Then when and if they have been repaired,
you must find the courage to let them go;
fly away, hopefully stronger than before.
If you have done well and their bellies are full of love,
just maybe they will be able to share what they have now,
with the next lost soul they meet along the ditch.
Just maybe, life may survive the waste and pollution
mankind has so carelessly left behind
to impede the advancement of mankind on the highway of life,
known as the ditch.

*The ditch is an expression I and other police
officers used to refer to the expressway.*

What is Marriage

Marriage is when two, who are in love,
bond into one, facing the world;
stronger than when they were as one.
Giving each other the strength,
necessary to weather the storms,
whatever they might be,
by leaning on each other.

Married people understand each other
by listening, and sharing problems,
no matter how trivial or large they might be.
Married people believe in each other,
when everything and everyone tells you it won't work.

Marriage is when you are apart,
but nothing can interfere with your love;
because the spirit of your love is always present
to chase those demons away.
Forgiving and understanding is the very essence
for the survival of marriage;
without forgiveness and understanding,
there is no marriage.

Marriage is commitment; unending commitment,
giving in to one another
without hesitation is all-important; a two way street.

In marriage, honesty is the very heart,
its core, if not there, there can be no marriage,
no foundation, on which to build the structure
necessary to house your love.

Believing in marriage, and love, is to believe in yourself,
because if you don't believe in yourself,
marriage and love, you can never be successful
at any of the above.

Michael Becker

5TH PRECINCT

PASSING MOMENTS

Christmas Gift

In days of old, I've been told.
Men much, much wiser than I
gave gifts that were not bought or sold.

The wondrous gifts came from the heart;
no production line was needed for these gifts.
They were not made of intricate parts.

These wise men each took hold of the others' hands.
The simple words they spoke were a Christmas gift;
With conviction and love, they took a firm stand.

Christmas gift, one might say, sounds a little empty.
Oh! How foolish; it was God's gift to us: his only son.
Through his Christmas gift, our lives are filled with plenty.

"Merry Christmas" is what is said today.
Gifts are given wrapped in pretty paper and bright bows.
I wonder what the wise of today, might think of yesterday.

His son lives, no matter how you hear it, or it is said;
And now he is gone from this earth,
but he fulfilled God's Christmas promise.
Through God's gift, so wondrously given,
we have eternal life, it is said.

Christmas Joy

Hello, my little sweet.
God, you're beautiful, and so complete.

I counted your little toes and fingers,
and found them so small in the palm of my hand.

The angels smiled down upon me,
the day God gave me your mother,

then once again when I walked her down the aisle,
to the altar, where I received a son.

With their gentle caring love,
they brought me to this day, where I met you, my love.

To some, you may seem a terror.
But to me, you will always be my little Kira.

Grandpa's sweet little love;
An angel from above.

My little bundle
of Christmas joy.

Michael Becker

What the Woods Means to Me

To listen to a squirrel chatter
in a far distant barren tree;
See a chipmunk scampering
through the multi-colored leaves;
Sunlight carving its way
through the bony fingers of the trees,
like cleansing rays from heaven.
To stand in their warm glow,
bathing you right down to your very soul,
Skipping a pebble across a babbling brook;
watching the rings left behind disappear,
as if you were never there.
Lifting a baby bird gently from the ground,
placing it back where it can be found,
Lying on my back in the soft leaves and clover,
inhaling their pungent aroma.
Looking at the lazy, billowy white soft underbelly
of the clouds moving above;
in his majestic royal blue sky.
Feeling all warm and full of love at peace inside--
that's what the woods means to me.

Down By the Lake

As I sit on the bank of the lake
Listening to a pair of loons
call to each other
across the dark lonely waters,
with their song of love,
I felt how wonderful,
in this crazy mixed up world,
two lovely creatures
can still find their way,
just by the song of love.
I watched the moon as it danced
its way upon the dark surface
of this tranquil, warm body of water,
making it seem
as if it were alive and performing
a waltz in the grand ballroom
for all the angels in their celestial seats
to see from high above.
I watched the waves come in
and kiss the beach,
as gently as a mother's lips
might caress her baby's soft tender skin,
then roll back out,
leaving only little lines in the sand,

Michael Becker

the only trace
that it had ever been there at all,
and I thought
how wonderful nature is
as it fills itself with glee
The soft scent of the pine,
carried in the wind,
comes to me from behind
and the sound of the rustling therein,
letting me know I'm still anchored
to this fertile earth,
part of all there is or ever will be;
how incredible to know that
you're part of all there is.
Then I catch the aroma
of a dying campfire,
and I think of all the loving creatures
back there waiting for me,
knowing I am wanted and needed,
but I must stay for just a little longer,
so I can fill my heart and mind
with what only Mother Nature
can fill me with;
letting me know I am one
with the universe.
When I rise, I pick up a stone,
and skip it across the surface of the lake's moonlit face,
where it comes to rest,
as it settles to the bottom,
like a baby returning to the womb,
feeling full, I turn and walk away,
into the dark shadows of the tall pines
along the path of life,
taking me home to where I belong.

Fourth of July

The smell of sulfur hung in the air,
sparks showered down as if,
water bursting through the narrows of a waterfall
thousands of feet above.
A single spark drifting down,
grasping onto life, like a lonely heartbeat,
over the golden-rods in the fields,
at dawns first gleaming.
Little children twirling sparklers with all the color of the rainbow,
shooting off sparks of honor,
to I wonder if they even know what or why.
Rockets setting the dark cloudless sky aglow,
showering sparks down upon us,
like from the kettles of the great steel mills back east,
letting us know of great things past and present.
The sound of fife and drum of off in the distance,
calling up memories of great deeds of men and women long ago
and as short as just around the last corner.
Old glory waving as she unfurls,
to withstand what stress might be placed upon her,
knowing she might faultier, but never fall,
no matter how raged and torn,
for the blood that has been shed
gives the strength to stand whatever the test.

Michael Becker

The fourth of July, some might say, just another day,
in the array of things great and small, not so,
it's a day to honor your dad and mine
and let's not forget the mothers and all the others,
that have bleed and died to make us free.
So let's all hold on to each other,
as the one family we were meant to be,
letting the rest of the world know,
no matter what color or how we speak,
what it's like to be free,
as standing naked before God in total unity.
The fourth of July is not just another day,
but the day that makes all other day's possible,
throughout this great land, we call home,
the land of the free and the brave, the one and only
U.S.A.

Hunt of the Nighthawk

To breeze through the fields at night,
the tall grass gently caressing my breast.
Dew drops leaving moisture upon my unclad legs,
seeing little animals scurry around on the ground,
little white tails bobbing all about.
Furry creatures of the night,
darting about from their fright.
To rise, to my high perch,
only to spring back down with the grace of a dove.
Rising up to shake the moisture from my face,
standing upon the ground,
looking at the sky filled with candlelight.
Now, after eating the morsels I had found,
I spread my wings to catch the night air and rise.
Looking to the east, I watch the birth of a new day.

Michael Becker

My Darling

As I look out the window this morning,
and see the bright sun-rays
playing their way across the fields of green
that lie just beyond,
I can't help but sense,
even though you're not even near,
the warmth that you provide from your inner glow,
the bright rays, make everything look so clean and new.
Not unlike the cleanliness that you make me feel,
from your mere existence
that radiates from your very soul.
I love spring; it's the time when all things are renewed,
the buds strain to burst open and spread their petals
to absorb the moisture of the early morning mist.
But it also makes me fearful,
that like that same mist, you will disappear,
as if burned away by the warm morning rays.
Life is so uncertain,
and we wonder if we will be lucky enough
to always hear the morning birds songs,
watch the butterfly as it dances on the light air currents
blown in on God's breath.
You are all those things and much more;
to lose you would be to lose all that is meaningful.
Without the wonderful mysteries of your beauty,
I would never have anything by which to compare spring;
the renewal of life.
You are life.

Spring

To watch a newborn fawn
in its attempt to stand;
To observe the petals of a flower
open to the soft warm rays of the sun.
To see raindrops run down the bent branch
from the weight of winter's snow,
until it comes to rest against a bud,
nourishing it to life.
To see a killdeer run across the ground
dragging it's wing;
To see an earthworm poke up its head
from fresh mounds of earth.
To lie and watch the grass grow,
while smelling the clover.
To watch the baby pheasants all in a line
follow mom down the fence row.
To see a squirrel peeking its head through the leaves
of its wintery nest.
To look at the soft underbelly of the clouds;
dark ones gone for now.
To be awakened in the morning
by many songs of birds.
By the early birds' song
To clasp the warm hand of another,
not the rough exterior of a glove.
To see God's promise of life
in the regeneration of spring.

Michael Becker

Superior

Setting on a sandy knoll,
I look out over the great lake.
Lightning flashes; I hear the rolling thunder,
as if a cannon fired on some far distant battlefield.

A storm approaches;
waves as dark as midnight, tipped with white,
curl back upon themselves,
giving the appearance of delicate lace,
Not unlike the hem of a wedding gown,
begin to crash against the rocky shore.

The surge of these great waves
tear chunks from the shore,
where sea and land meet as if in a lovers quarrel.
The same shore, that they once caressed,
as if in the kiss of two lovers,
gently embrace in the heat of passion.
Trees toppled, as boulders
are tossed and thrown about,
giving the appearance of a domestic quarrel;
Turning what was once a neat and tidy home,
into complete and utter disarray.

But there came an end, to the fury,
as there always does in lovers quarrels.
A time of healing begins,
the lake smooths out, calm like a mirror,
reflecting God's heaven above.

As I sat there pondering
over what had just occurred
and what I had observed, lessons were learned.
I knew without a doubt,
why they called this great lake
Superior.

The Pine

A pine of simple green
was standing all alone.
A storm came up and blew so hard
the tree became battered and torn.

A mighty bolt of lightning flashed
and struck the heart of that tree,
causing it to blow apart,
never more to be.

Wait, what is this I see at the base
of where it used to be?
Why, it's a baby tree.

When uncle John read this.
He said that is just how it would be.
God love him.

Michael Becker

Time

The sun coming up in the morn,
casting shadows across the face of history.
A glacier moving methodically over the tillable soil,
turning it to barren waste.
Atoms growing and moving, creating and destroying
in the never ending change of things.
A seed slowly molded into a vivacious life,
only to be snuffed out in a millisecond; gone forever.
Time is wasted when there is no productivity.
Time is forgotten when there is no history.
Time is nothing without knowledge.
Ages come, ages go; time lives on forever:
sad, lonely, forgotten, happy times.
The time of a man's life is but the blink of a gnat's eye.
Measure man not by the time he has been here,
but by the goals and accomplishments he has achieved.
Time can slip through your fingers like the elusive waterfall,
tumbling to its sure and sudden death.
We must stand as the proverbial sentinel,
so that time may never be stolen away.

6TH PRECINCT

THOUGHTS & FEELINGS

Alone and Used Up
I felt

Oh my love, as you can see,
I've tried so hard for you and me.
I'm used and burnt from the fires
Just to be here with you, my love.

Now here I am, by your side,
with no other place to hide;
Take me in your arms, I plead,
Hold me, make me whole again.

I don't care if at times we live in sin;
It's the only time it feels like heaven.
Look at you, then look at me;
Without you, I'm nothing the world can see.

In your embrace is where I long to be
Setting my whole being free.
So we can soar up high and dance
with our hearts so full of glee.

I love you, angel; that's plain to see;
I thought all things that matter had come to an end.
Then, my love, you stepped in,
and I found it was time for new love to begin.

Blind

Feel the sun upon my face.

Dip my hands into a cool mountain stream.

Hear the song of a lark.

The whispering of the wind.

As it dances through the boughs of the pines.

The smell of wilted flowers.

Yes even the aroma of the dirt, of which we came.

How many times have you seen these things?

Yet you say I am blind.

Michael Becker

Completion

The early signs of life shine through my window,
and I wonder what new adventures will occur today.
Is it cloudy, like my mind? Or is it dark, like my soul?
As I contemplate
stepping outside, a thought occurs.
Will today be the day when your love
brings out the soft chirps of the sparrows?
Will today be the day when your charm
flourishes the tulips?
Or will today be like the rest,
dark, cold and mysterious, like the feelings I have?
The time passes me by, and as I step outside,
my eyes wither.
Nothing is in sight.
I see only
a single star slowly diminish away,
leaving no trace of life.
I feel the sorrow and agony;
you then appear.
Having wished for this moment for all eternity,
a subtle sense of wonder arises.
Stepping away, out of your light,
I look up, and that one star that slowly died
twinkles more brightly than ever before.
I now know that my day is not like the others.
I don't need you, or the sense of failure.
I have this star.
She knows how I am feeling,
and fulfills every needing desire.
Stepping back inside, I now know
that I have, want and need....
Completion.

End of Day

You like a breath of fresh air;
I have to admit in this entire world,
there is no one quite like you.
When I'm with you,
it seems you flatten out the tallest of mountains,
making it possible for me to pass
with very little difficulty.
Your words are as the birds songs are to my ear,--
ever so soothing, always bringing me total peace.
Your warm embrace, reminds me of the warm glow
of the crackling flame of the hearth,
as daylight slips over the rim of Mother Earth,
bring on the chills of night.
When I watch you move,
it's as if we're the breeze, as it gently dances
through the soft green grass at water's edge.
And when I look into your eyes,
I find they're not only wide, but deep as well;
I find myself wishing
I could be drawn into them,
where here I would be able to float
in the heated waters of your very soul,
Feeling the waves of your incredible spirit
slap against me.
All in all, I don't believe that there is anyone in all the world
that I would rather come home to
and lie down with than you,
At the end of the day.

Michael Becker

Evil That Plays in the Heart

When I see you,
my heart is filled with evil thoughts.

Thoughts that play in my heart,
are forever urging me on,
to do what some might think are vile wicked deeds.

I find myself without fear,
unable to hold those thoughts back
when I'm with you.

Instead, I feel I can hide them
in the glare of your all-consuming beauty,
which blinds all who attempt to look in your direction.

You're the only drink that can quench this thirst I have,
and conceivably still the fires that burn deep in my loins.

Your love is full of compassion;
as full as the oceans of the world are with water,
constant and precious.

All who know you take refuge in the warm glow
of your all-inspiring love.

To know you is to drink from the rivers of your delight;
I would not feel the least bit vanquished,
if I were to perish in your arms.

For I would know, as I slipped from this earth,
it would be in the embrace of love,
the most wondrous love of all.
Your love.

Words not Bullets

Hear Me

Hear me!
Listen to my plea;
don't turn away from me in this time of distress.
Bend down your ear
and give me speedy answers filled with love.
For my days disappear like smoke rising
from the warm ember coals of a dying campfire.
My health is broken and my heart is sick.
It has been trampled,
as the grass under the hooves of the herd
from the past that is withered.
My life is passing swiftly, as the evening shadows
that cross the white- tipped mountains of the west.
To be cut down in mid-life,
shortening my days.
I cry out, don't let me die halfway through my years.
Let my light stretch to the far ends of the earth.
So my shadow will not fall short.
But I shall perish like the worn-out clothing
that is discarded and thrown aside.
Gone like the mist playing its way across a pond,
burned away by the hot sun of the new day.

Michael Becker

I am

I am not a mythical fairy or prince,
I am not a movie hero in a white hat;
I am real, filled with fire and lightning;
I am honesty, filled with self-worth;
I am not Stonehenge, heartless and unfeeling;
I am not masked, in the world of falsehood.
I am a man that cries and feels pain;
I am the one that stands naked for the entire world to see.
Although born fatherless, I am not a lying bastard;
I am, I pray, truth pure and simple;
I am the one who reaches out,
for the good of others, through his pain;
I am not one, though, who dwells on his pain;
I am not some fool that hides in the corner;
I am the one who reaches for the stars and beyond.
I am a believer in my meager existence;
I am everything, and I am nothing.
You ask what I am;
It's simple--I am whatever
I am.

Kiss

A honest kiss is something no one should miss,

filling your heart with heavenly bliss,

as soft and tender as petals on a flower,

giving you strength and tremendous power.

The kiss is a way of showing you care,

one wonderful way of clearing the air.

Michael Becker

Loss I think not

In this world of disbelief
It's so hard to think
To feel
I have
You

You
Are all
Things
There are
In this world to believe in

What in God's name is left?
When you disappear
Like a puff of smoke
At life's
End

End
I think not.
You, like life or love,
are the very beginning of
beginnings.

Beginnings
of love, life, happiness
Today and everyday
thereafter
with no disasters.

Music

Music is like water rushing over a waterfall;

Children's voices laughing in the night;

A leaf flipping gently upon the ground.

The sun brings the earth to life in the early morn,

Beyond, to even a higher note, it's Gods smile upon his face.

Love, touching our hearts, giving ever lasting peace and grace.

Music, what a wonderful thing it is;

from the powerful thunder to the gentle rain,

from sorrow all around, to loving peace inside waiting to be found.

Michael Becker

My Heart

I have a question that has been plaguing me
far too long.
Of what value am I, if any at all?
Do I deserve to be part of this great creation?
Does anybody care what I might say,
value what I have learned,
or even hear the advice I might give?
Why should they? Look at me I'm nothing
but a dried up weed in the garden of life.
I wonder, is there anyone who really wants me around?
What fun am I? I'm not even good to look at.
I love everyone so much, but does it really matter?
Should I love others as I do?
I don't even see, feel or smell love in the air for me.
I feel like I'm opaque, someone that is looked right through,
so another can enjoy the view beyond,
never even noticing me there.
Well at least I don't block the view and irritate others that way.
Is there anyone who I can hold,
so I might feel the warmth of love,
look into their eyes and see something more
than pity looking back?

Night Shadows

I sat in the warm glow of the campfire,
looking across the flames,
as if staring into space,
and what I saw were the flames dancing
as they threw shadows across her golden skin.
Even in this dim light, I could see her beauty radiating
its warmth into the cool of the night.
Her hair looked like spun silk, all aglow from the flames,
making it appear as if she wore a halo.
She had eyes that sparkled like two jewels,
that illuminated the pathway home,
to her loving heart.
When she spoke, it was as a whisper;
I believe that all the little creatures
in the forest itself held their breath.
The fire was warm, the feeling was right
as she rose from the fire
and walked into the shadows of the night.
I felt passion and emotion
flow from my body and soul, like a slow death.
then once again with pain,
slowly the return of life and my breath.

Michael Becker

Rose Colored Glasses

I don't mean to diminish the anguish or pain
that the ones we care about feel from time to time.
There are those that might even say
that I look at the world through rose colored glasses,
and maybe that's so,
but I would rather put on those rose-colored glasses
and go search for the good in the world,
than be like those that murmur and complain,
only seeing the bad and the ugly
that they perceive is always present around them.
If by chance that is all you see,
it is a sorry, sorry world you live in,
sorry, sorry indeed.
So how can you find the good
and suppress the evil that lurks,
not only in the dark, but the bright of day?
Come with me, put on those rose colored glasses,
so that we might distinguish the difference,
seeing through whatever might try to blind us,
turning us away from the right path.
Together we can turn away the bad and the ugly,
walk in the bright sun's rays,
enjoying the good that is all around us.
By doing so, someday we might be able to lay
those rose-colored glasses down for good.

You'll Always Have Me

When you're feeling happy and think you might explode,
you'll always have me, to keep the bubble afloat.

When you're feeling sad and you really want to cry,
you'll always have me, to tell those tears bye-bye.

When you're feeling lost and can't find your way back,
you'll always have me, to keep you on the right track.

When you're in need of a friend, someone just to talk to,
you'll always have me, that other ear, just for you.

When you're feeling lonely and don't know what to do,
you'll always have me, to bring the sun out for you.

When you're feeling you have made a mistake
and think no one will forgive you,
you'll always have me, to believe in you.

When you're caught in a lie and think you can't be trusted,
you'll always have me, the one who has faith in you.

So no matter how you're feeling,
no matter what you have done,
you'll always have me there for you, hun.

Michael Becker

7TH PRECINCT

LOSS & LONLINESS

Death of the Midway

The sounds of joy and laughter have all faded away.
But that's the way it is when no one is left on the midway.
Dinosaurs, giants that once roamed the land,
are now slowly dismembered by human hand.
The colored lights that once burned bright,
one by one blink out, in the cold of the night,
the music becomes still.
No one is left on the carousel,
to reach out for that magical gold ring.
Little wooden horses become still; they look so lifeless,
it fills my body with a cold chill.

Bent and crooked with a pointed stick,
a little old man walks ever so slow,
picking up what lays upon the ground,
hoping to beat the coming snow.
His heart is heavy and laden, filled with grief,
All the children are gone, he would like to stay.
But he can't, for you see;
he has just witnessed the death of the midway.

For The Love of God

With quivering lips tears are held back,
composure to regain,
makes one wish,
they had never seen her pain.
One more time you know
you have let her down,
which makes you feel like that
mangy old hound.
You spring back up to your feet
to take her in your arms,
praying you have not been
the cause of much more harm.
Letting her down
seems to be quite a regular thing,
you wonder why she stays
when nothing to the home you bring.
Misery, illness, legs that won't hold me up,
quite a frail man,
what she has been dealt is
really a miserable hand.
Sometimes you wish you could let her go,
but you find you are too selfish,
which makes you feel that you are rather low.
She surely does love you, God only knows why,
but for the love of God,
why don't I?

Michael Becker

Goodbye

Goodbye I say once more,
knowing we must part.
Taking with you once again
a little more of my heart.

It's funny how two bodies pass
on life's stormy sea.
To come together a brief moment
never more to be.

Love is but a flighty thing;
it flutters all about.
All the powers on this earth
can never put it out.

Oh my love, you must know,
even though I have never said;
the thoughts I have
that fill my heart and head.

If you should disappear and be gone,
only the memory of my love for you
would give me the power to carry on,

To do the things that must be done,
until we are once again united,
and stand together as one.

Life of Sadness with Bright Moments

In this life of sadness,
It's nice to meet someone so full of gladness,

whose words flow like honey,
always willing to give of her plenty.

With eyes that shine with glee,
like they were shining only for me.

Words, she speaks with tender poise,
never attempting to just make noise.

So beautiful a creature has ever graced the eyes of man;
I doubt there ever will again.

Michael Becker

Loss

A flower from my garden has blown away;

Never again will its fragrance brighten my day.

It leaves a dark and cheerless spot where it used to belong;

This gardener's hoe has come to rest.

In his heart, he knows he has lost one of his very best.

Michael

Michael has been there;
he has run through the streets barefoot.
he has tried every desperate attempt
to get rid of the pain.
Michael has cried real tears;
he has let them fall from his hazel eyes,
and soak his blue-black hair.
He's been there;
Michael has felt it.
He has stood in the midst of his agony;
He has called out, expecting no one to hear;
But someone did hear.
Someone heard who has been there;
Someone who felt the pain, as he had felt the pain;
Someone who has run through the streets barefoot with him;
who has held him in the midst of his agony.

Michael Becker

Missing You

The sun was gliding slowly across the heavens.
As it embarked on its slow decent
toward the far distant rim of Mother Earth,
where it would disappear from a golden-red sky
at the conclusion of a perfect day.

The heavens filled with countless clouds,
I lay on the bank of a slow meandering river,
staring out at the sparkling surface as it passed by;
wondering what might lie just beneath the surface.

The river, nudging my memory,
reminded me of all the mysteries
that lay beneath your golden soft skin.
I once again found myself,
wishing you were by my side,
to comfort this tired old body.

You, like the settling sun,
have a way of bringing out the best in me,
just by your soothing ways.

There is not a day that goes by
I don't think of you in one way or another.
You are life on a cloudy day, heaven on any given day.

Missing you.

Words not Bullets

Never Enough

Giving her things I hoped would be of value
as we traveled through life,
but it was never enough;
Liking her, not just loving her, above all the rest,
but it was never enough.
Working harder than the other guy, so I might earn her respect,
but it was never enough.
Myself, I always gave whatever I had,
but it was never enough.
Listening the best I could, with everything pouring in around me,
but it was never enough.
Talking and sharing all my thoughts,
but it was never enough.
Caring about all her problems big and small,
but it was never enough.
Through life I always prayed, whatever the pain she could bear it,
but it was never enough.
Asking her to forgive, the truth was the only way,
but it was never enough.
Forgiving the transgressions, no matter the pain,
but it was never enough.
Watching her drive away, praying, not knowing if she would return,
but it was never enough.
Sacrificing, so she might have,
but it was never enough;
It simply was not, not ever enough for her.
I just know, deep down inside, I could have done so much more.
What I gave was but a pinch of sand in the hourglass of time.
When the final curtain descends,
the veil of darkness draws in tight upon me,
I am received by the dark, loveless land
of the constant arctic wind,
where the only shelter I might find
will be the blue cold walls of an ice cave,
I will have received my just reward, for never doing enough.

Michael Becker

Only the Lonely

There once was a song,
only the lonely know the feeling I feel.
Well, that doesn't even begin to express
what it is like when you have lost everything.
Lonely is just a part,
not even touching the reality of the loss in life,
the loss of everything we hold near and dear.
When you're young and full of all the right stuff,
you know, the things that dreams are made of,
knowing it will last forever,
you are unconquerable as a king.
Then the enlightenment that only comes with age,
begins to shine, lighting up the rocky roads
that you now find yourself on.
But even then, you stumble and fall,
tripping you up are all sorts of things--
the list could go on forever.
When I saw the fire go out in your eyes
was the worst time of all,
knowing I had lost all that was the essence of manhood.
Without manhood,
there is no way for me to bring out
all the glory of your womanhood.
You know, you haven't just lost your dignity,
but have been robbed of everything
that makes the one you love whole.
Then life slowly begins to crumble all around you,
you know you are nothing,
sitting back, you think of all the thoughts
and lost dreams you wanted to share
with the one you held most dear.
Only the lonely know the feeling I feel;
I wish being lonely was all I felt that was bad,
being nothing is like being alone in a dark space,
seeing all that's around you,
but feeling nothing at all.

Shadow Dancers

As I see it, homeless children
are but shadow dancers on the wall,
Lost souls in the murky land,
on the fuzzy edge of reality.

Dying children, that mourn the dead,
living with adults, un-kept, un-fed.
From the cradle to the table, no one to care,
no one hardly knowing they were even there.

Sorrow shown in the eyes by the many tears that flow,
that have lost the bright light of their youthful glow.
Teeter totters, swing sets sit silent, no laughter in the park,
children that once played there have now lost their spark.

Shadow dancers, made to move, by the finger puppeteers,
on the wall, throughout their young formative years.
This might be alright with most women and man,
but I think it's time for intervention from the Master's hand.

Going to bed, hungry, wet, sick, unkempt,
un-fed, alone, and always on the verge of tears,
Dreams they have very few, nightmares plenty,
all these things, they will suffer throughout the years.

Michael Becker

Tears

Tears are nature's gentle rain,
which wash away
the pain and sorrow
from ones soul,
cleaning the windows;
letting joy,
like a bright sunray
come in
to warm one's inner being.

Tears in the Moon Light

Silky and warm,
A tear slides down
Caught in a moonbeam;
settled in a pool of sadness.

My manhood delicate;
Strong but yet fragile,
As it becomes lost
In instinctive fate,
Hurt and unforgiving;

Unable to enter its shelter;
unable to have the strength
To break through to a safe harbor;
Unable to break the net,
alone to bear the coldness,
Alone for all to see, he hardly stands
Unable to pass on his seed.

His manhood, not like the pack,
Must now live the life of a lone wolf;
Limp and unforgiven;
To be embraced by solitude;
Coldness always his only friend;
Not to catch him, but to help him fall.

Once strong as an oak,
Now weak as a rose;
In his thoughts, he tries to suppress
The sadness and emptiness
Trying to hide the beat
Of the lone wolf's heart.

Michael Becker

The Inner Me

On the outside, to everyone I appear
happy and full of life.
No one, thank God, can see how I am dealing
with my inner strife.
Filled with pain all the day long,
I know this pain will never be gone;
Feeling like I'm less than a man.
unable to do all that the rest can.
able to love within my mind,
only to fail at love all the time.
On the outside, I know I look good;
That's the way it should.
When I wake my arms hurt so bad.
Letting anyone know would make me sad.
I'm hardly able to rise from my bed.
It's best that to all whom I know this is left unsaid.
And those I love can only see
the bright, happy outer me.
I would never want them to see
how sad and lonely is the inner me.

The Passing

A rare exotic flower has perished from my garden,
A flower I cherished above the rest.
Her beauty and fragrance will never again grace my senses;
This flower has been ripped away.
I stand with hoe in hand, not knowing
if it is salty tears or sweat I feel
running down my hard-worked, worn face.
Being a gardener is no easy life,
knowing all things of beauty in life.
come with great risk.
But the loss of the most delicate of flowers
is always hardest.
I will miss the color
that is now a dark corner in my heart
where she used to belong.
It feels as if the warmth from the sun
has been stolen away,
even on the brightest of summer days.
Alone I must stand to face the coming nightfall,
and the passing of each pursuing day.
Cold is the dark wind
that brings the loneliness of night.

Michael Becker

We All Need Hugs

Once I was a fair specimen of humanity;
I stood out among the best.
But I was homosexual, bisexual;
or had a bad blood transfusion, a bad needle,
maybe just loved the wrong person.
Now I sit in the dark,
shunned from society; an outcast.
I could have been a mother, a father,
brother, sister, son or daughter.
I have lost so much, no one will come close.
What's so sad is that what I have
can't be passed on by casual touch,
or even sharing the air we breathe.
My heart hasn't stopped feeling;
I still care about what is going on around me.
People around me are so smug,
why don't they know, even I need hugs.

Your Presence

Loneliness started the day I looked deep into your eyes,
and is only abated when you are near.
Loneliness is felt most, when you depart,
walking away, taking with you small parts of my heart.
If waking, I found you nowhere in sight,
God only knowing how long it would be
before I would be with you again,
Not knowing when I would feel the warmth of your presence
or the pleasure of your company,
I am sure it would be the beginning of my end.
Loneliness is when the warmth of your voice,
music to my ears, is no longer there.
The kindness I see reflected
in the most beautiful portrait known to man,
your face, would be missing.
The rhythm of your breathing,
which brings my room to life--gone forever.
Most of all, the warmth that surrounds me,
from the angelic glow
that comes from your heavenly form,
that penetrates my very soul,
would turn cold.
Missing all of this, I am sure, I would surely die.
What would be left, but a wide chasm, dark void, a total vacuum,
that no mortal man could survive.

Michael Becker

If I were not to perish, life would be worse,
to live without your presence, being
surrounded by caring people would be meaningless.
You are my morning, my very beginning,
the essence of everything that tells me I am alive.
The reason for my next breath, my every feeling good or bad,
why I reach out or turn my back on this fragile world.
Without you, there would be no tomorrows,
the evening shades would descend, the final curtain fall.
I would play out the last scene, mountains would explode,
fire would rain down from the sky, ending all time as I knew it.
I truly hope you know and feel how important you are.
If your little feet had never been placed on this earth,
what a loss that would have been to mankind.
You must know that every word you utter, every look you give,
has a profound effect on all those around you.
You must be a gift sent from heaven, one of the very special people
that come along once in a while,
making this world a better place by your presence.

Who Cares

When things don't go quite the way you would like,
You start looking inside yourself and begin to wonder,
or at least ask what went wrong. Is it just me?
Thinking oh, I'm just offensive to be around,
or they really don't give a damn,
That's why all my friends took off on the lam.
Well, who can really blame them?
Most of the time I don't even like myself,
So why should anyone else?
I guess all I can do is live this life from within,
letting the rest of the world pass by.
If someone needs me,
just go ahead and use me as you wish.
Then toss me away like the disposable can,
along the freeway of life.
Oh, if I'm lucky, I might help someone once in a while,
Say something nice or even worthwhile or of value,
Maybe even write something that has meaning,
but does it really matter?
When the true test, the test of time has passed,
who will really care that I was even here
or passed by?
Nobody. Not even me.

Written when I became sick
And thought I had lost EVERYTHING

Michael Becker

8TH PRECINCT

DREAMS

Balance

I dreamed a dream once,
that all the vile hate was taken from this earth,
and all that was left was the beauty
of God's great and wondrous love.
It seemed on face value to be the greatest of gifts,
but alas it threw the gears of life
completely out of balance.
We became lazy and carefree,
there was no competition or drive left,
because there was no need for it.
Then love its very self
became a silly and boring game,
no winners or losers,
no meaning or direction.
When I awoke, I thanked the Lord
for hate, contempt, and distrust.
For without them,
we mortals would not know what love,
trust, and compassion even meant.
Because you see,
for every action there is a reaction,
without one, it's impossible to have the other.
Hate is so terrible;
I'm so glad for love,
and that I have lived long enough
to know the difference.

Dreams

I was thinking of us, my love, last night,
And the few times we shared--
How good we and they were
But now, my love, we are apart,
yet we still hold in our heart
Dreams.

For in our dreams, we are
Locked together as one
Holding hands on satin sheets,
talking all night under the
Silver moon
Kissing and holding each other tight,
in dreams--

for no matter the distance
or the obstacle,
I will always belong to you,
for we are meant for each other
not only in reality, but also in our
dreams.

Michael Becker

I Wish

I wish I could hear you speak words of esteem,
gentle and kind.
I wish I could feel your warm and tender body
lying next to mine.
I wish I could feel the warmth of your breath caress my neck,
from your soft passionate whispers.
I wish I could feel your moist, luscious lips
as they gently tugged upon my earlobe.
I wish I could feel your pearly white teeth
playfully nibble on my breast.
I wish I could feel your soft, silky hands
gently glide up and down as you caressed my hips.
I wish I could look deep in your eyes
only to see your loving stare, no pain hidden there.
I wish I could join together with you as one,
so I could feel your heart beat with mine.
I wish I could feel love deep in my soul,
love that could only come from your heavenly glow.
I wish I could feel once again whole, of value and worth,
but I believe, for me, it's not to be.
I wish I could have that feeling one feels when one has given
all they have from within, once again.
I wish I could be locked together in the embrace of love,
at the moment I depart
to meet my maker, the one up above.
I wish I could feel when I arrive up above,
what it would be like to walk hand in hand
with an angel like you, so full of love.

Words not Bullets

My Dream Lover

The wind whispers your name in caressing waves,
as I walk alone, remembering your silken touch.
A tear slowly appears, cold against my cheek,
and I ache for your tender touch;
one last finger trailing my spine,
One last wave of passion flowing through my body.
The hair on my body rises;
even the thought of you excites me to a frenzy.
But, I must cool the embers,
Let the fire smolder
'til I can add fuel to the flames.
Sadness approaches;
the wind howls,
sending pleasure through me again;
a longing only you can satisfy;
I am the only one who knows
my dream lover
who comes to me in my dreams,
departing with the morning shadows.
Out of the darkness she came, long hair flowing;
eyes shining, with pleasure burning,
and it was all consuming,
the knowing of what was there,

Michael Becker

I felt it flowing through
the silken touch of her hands upon my soul.
The desire was all consuming;
The night was long and passionate,
and my dreams restless.
The dawn was spawned to soon,
Chasing away
the shadows which held her captive,
and now I walk,
the wind howling at my heels,
my dream lover following in
the shadows,
Whispering in silence.
And I remember her tender touch,
My dream lover.

Shadows

In the shadows of the night,
I walked without the help of light.
I walked in search of what might have been
Had I not lived this life from within.
This walk, I walk alone,
and no one else can help me,
I got here on my own.
When I walked in the light,
I walked with my soul uptight,
Never fearing what the night might bring.
Now here I am, all alone,
searching for what might have been.
At the end of the shadows,
I see a faint glow.
Walking, stumbling; groping,
I finally step into the light of day.
Then I see that all I have had is a dream,
of what might be, if I had not been.

Michael Becker

Soul Mates

We met once, as if by chance;
we never dated nor did we dance.
We looked into each other's eyes,
without deception or disguise.
A silent message passed between;
your hungry heart was plainly seen.
You saw raw desire I could not hide;
You looked at me and saw inside.

How could one glance have said so much?
And caused a chill without a touch?
What was the chemistry of that night
that promised what we felt was right?
What satisfaction we'd have missed,
if we had not felt that heavenly bliss?
I know not if it was you,
or was it I who said, "Let's do".
But on that day, our souls were bare
As surely as our bodies there.

I knew our bodies would move in harmony;
a time I couldn't tell you apart from me.
Our minds, locked in passion as we were,
I felt my sense of time began to blur.
I felt I must have known you from before;
how else could you have reached my very core?
In a life perhaps before this one
what had we shared? What had we done?
With what I felt, emotions vast,
I must have loved you in the past.

But for now we go our separate ways,
To different lives, throughout our days.
I keep you though within my heart and dreams,
Eternal soul mates for all time, it seems.

Wishing For Love

As I watch the pale smoke rise
from the hot sparkling embers of a dying campfire.
I hear the laughter of friendship, as it is snuffed out,
like darkness tightening its grip, on day's last light,
Plunging us into the cold of the night.
I think how fragile love is,
blown and buffeted by the cold breeze,
to be lost to the dark,
not unlike the rays of light, at days end.
Love is as beautiful as the butterfly
that dances on multi-colored wings,
elusive as the grasshopper,
trying to escape the grasp of a small child at play.
To be caressed by love,
is like being brushed by lightning; energizing,
but yet on the edge of disaster.
Being filled with love
is as comforting as a baby
suckling on a mother's breast
but to be filled with love,
you have to willing to empty yourself completely.
I wish I could feel the pain of smoke against my nostrils,
abate the light at days end,
dance with the butterfly,
catch the grasshopper,
be caressed by lighting
and brush my lips across the breast of motherhood.
That I might empty myself of this pent up loneliness,
I have felt inside to long,
causing love to come rushing in,
filling me completely.

Michael Becker

9TH PRECINCT

WORDS

D.D. T'S

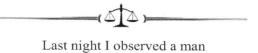

Last night I observed a man
who did not have his life quite in hand.
He said the doctor's name was Jarvis, an ant,
working inside with his team.
Heart surgery was his specialty,
jewelry he did on the side.
Making gold watch bobs was no problem;
he got the gold from
living or dead men and women's teeth.
Wait, wait, what is it? Oh, oh ok!
I need some blood; they've made a mistake.

I guess when you drink
and don't give a damn about your life,
you are going to have to learn to deal with its strife.
He is going to lose his wife,
family, dogs, and even his house,
most probably end up being a louse.

Inspired by a friend Chuck
Who lost the final battle

Midnight

Midnight is the bewitching hour, so I've been told,
A time when you have to hold on to all you behold.

Things move through the dark; dangerous things,
that no one can see.
Little things and large,
that are out there to destroy you and me.

Is it the wind, or a soft whisper that I hear?
Coaxing us from our safe place, it seems so very near.

If we step beyond the lights' warm glow,
From beyond the dark veil, we will we return, only God can know.

Midnight is filled with all kinds of dark and sinister forces.
They are out there to direct us on all the wrong courses.

You might think that the loss of life
is the worst that can happen.
Oh how wrong you would be.
If that were all, you would be clapping.
No, a cold hand can come out of the dark,
taking you by the throat;
Dragging you into the dark pits of hell,
on a sour note.

But you know, as bad as life may sometimes seem,
Love is there, like a beacon, giving off a bright gleam.

True love, I've been told, can conquer all.

Michael Becker

Thanks

Once in a while I feel completely lost.
Then I think of your soft and tender eyes.
Of which, I wish I could be absorbed, within.
The kind words that pass your exquisite lips.
The way you stand, your hands upon your hips.
Crisp cool air as it flips your hair,
Making me wish you were always there.
Most of all, that incredible, impish little smile
that is always there to brighten my day;
a smile that lights up the darkest corners of my soul;
Bringing me back from the land of the lost,
And enabling me to press on to greater goals.
If there are angels in heaven, one has gotten loose,
and has come down to me to graze the landscape.
Truly at times, I feel like I live in the cold ice caves
of the north, where the only warmth I have,
are the icy fingers
that play with my heart.
But the only true warmth I receive
is yours and yours alone.

Things You May Want to Live By

When you love,
love unconditionally.
When you give,
give with all that's in you.
When you praise,
let it flow from the heart.
Always look for the best in others,
nothing less would do.
When you give,
accept nothing in return;
If you expect something in return,
you gave nothing at all.
Communication means listening
as well as speaking, maybe more.
Honesty is the very heart of all that matters.
Honor all things,
life most of all.
When giving your word, keep it;
it's like gold.
Love and light give you the strength
and courage to meet the day.
Believe in a higher power;
life without belief is meaningless.
Never look back;
correct and move on.
A bird waits out the storm, his wing being his protection,
man waits out the storm, patience being his wing.
Sex is an act of giving,
validated from the pleasing quality of love.
Think of all men as equal,
and you won't mind looking in the looking glass.
Who we are is the sum of all we believe.

Michael Becker

To Whom It May Concern

Whether tomorrow comes or not, I would like to give thanks for however brief a moment I might spend in this great creation.

Being received by two loving parents willing to give of their all, so that a youngster might have the time to dream of the future uninhibited by the pressures of today.

For the gift of a woman, who took a boy's dreams, cultivating them into the reality of manhood, willing to share the joy with the misery, but always having the capability of making him feel as if he were on top of the world.

A child with truth and peace written in her eyes and an incredible smile, lighting my heart with her every action, lifting me high in a way that only a father can feel, from that wonderful surge of energy that comes from the youthful example the young can give by being the way they are.

For a wonderful son, received by just giving away, one of my most prized possession, thank you; now I have two children, which are more valuable than all riches man may bestow upon me and worth more than life itself.

Having the opportunity to share what little I have with other creatures that I have walk the path of life with, for the laughter, smiles, and even the tears, for without them I would not have felt the things necessary to know one has lived.

Started in 1979, where my thanks will stop God only knows.
As long as he wants me here I will by giving thanks.

Thoughts

1. How can man when he looks at universe, in all its splendor, be so conceited that he believes, that he is all there is?

2. How can we like black and red licorice and all the colors of the gumballs, but think all those around us are tasteless?

3. We all have needs, and needs have us all.

4. To see the spark of wisdom in a child's eyes is as wonderful as knowing the sun will surely rise.

5. For one to be imperfect is to be perfect. Be proud of your imperfection, without them there is nothing to work for: no goals, no tomorrows.

6. Pain lets you know you're alive; love makes it bearable.

7. The sweat of work, is nectar of the Gods.

8. If someone likes you, cherish it. If they love you, beware. If they like and love you, be thankful.

9. Living is when you are willing to give all you have, that is necessary to sustain life to those around you, because without those around you, life would be meaningless, and of no value.

10. Without God there is no love; what you would feel would be lust, greed, envy, selfishness, all meaningless emotions with no direction or worth.

11. Life is so wonderful if your cup is full, but for your cup to be full, you have to be willing to empty it at a moment's notice.

12. When I stretch myself as thin as possible is when I feel the fullest.

Michael Becker

13. Life without hugs; who wants it?

14. Dying is just a passing moment. To die without honor is forever.

15. The bird puts his head under his wing to wait out the storm; man must wait out the storm, patience being his wing.

16. Lonely is the night that brings the cold wind, blowing through the cracks and crannies, of this flimsy shelter of which I set within.

17. As I look out at the bones scattered all about this land, whether made from rust or decaying marrow, I wonder what has happen to all the mighty that once ruled this earth.

18. Man is a hodgepodge of many things.

19. Wisdom like grass, gently caressed by the wind, must be nurtured, nurtured to learn how to bend.

20. For one to feel and express courage, one must first feel the pain of fear; without fear, courage is meaningless.

21. Life is an accumulation of bitter herbs, which it takes to make delectable delights.

22. Anger is like a rubber band, when flung out, it snaps back with equal force, and nothing is gained.

23. Love is the most precious gift I have to give, so take from it as you wish, but remember, when it's gone, it's just an empty dish.

24. Love is waking in the night, to find a tear upon her cheek, to wipe it away, hold her tight, letting her know everything is all right.

His Tool

On March 7th, 2011 I lost my darling wife Sheila to lung cancer. It was and is one of the hardest times in my life I ever went through. I was so mad at God I hardly knew what to do.

Well I struggled along until October. Then I was invited to a Halloween get together at a state park in Michigan, where I met a man who was having a very hard time, thinking he was no good and wanted to walk out into the lake, to never come back. Well, this set up a moment in time that I would like to share with you.

When someone is in trouble, I feel we can't turn our back, and I didn't. We started to talk about the power of God and how much God loved him and wanted to help him. I also told him I loved him; that he was my brother and how important he was to God. We talked about his children, his wife, his church and so much more. I guess the overall theme was God's love. We both came to tears many times.

What was so wonderful was I am not gifted with a great knowledge of how God's plan works. No, not me. What is so wonderful is when you walk with our creator and become his tool. Then we open our mouth, he fills it with all the words we need to accomplish his will. God never lets us down.

We talked for hours, this wonderful child of God and I. When we were done, I felt he was thinking better of himself and all that was around him. As we parted I asked him that when he got home tonight, ask his wife to get down on her knees and join him in prayer. Then to pray with all his heart of where he, as a man wanted to go with his life as she listen to his prayer. That was how we parted on that dark night.

Michael Becker

Now, my dear friends, I want to tell you how I felt as I looked back at that night. At the beginning, I told you how mad I was at God.

Well that feeling began to disappear. As I talked with that man God was working on me and my anger, because as I poured out my love the anger went with it. God's love came rushing in taking away the foolish thoughts I had deep inside me. I knew Sheila was where she was meant to be, and I felt I would see her some wonderful day.

Most important I was not alone; God was with me and always would be.

Please my dear friends, when God calls upon you, turn yourself over to him. Be his tool! You will never regret it, and when you feel most lost give yourself over to your best friend, God. He will do the rest.

I am back in step with the best friend I will ever have. Please walk with me my dear friends. I need you as well as I need my Lord.

Michael Becker

Words to Ponder

Life is without a doubt, as you grow older, a very lonely place to be. It is like you are in a prison and everything you value is on the outside, being reflected back in upon you.

I feel as if each and every day that passes, a little more of my soul is stripped away, leaving me with very little of what was once me.

You find it almost impossible to find someone to share, your thoughts with. Then when you do, you can't help but wonder if you will offend them, driving them away because of your inability to communicate without opening up you heart, revealing your darkest secrets.

Secrets you could only share with someone you trusted with your very life itself, the essence of all of what and who you are. That person would have to be filled with the very essence of all you held in your heart to be true and wholesome; a person with unending depth, knowledge and understanding.

That person would also be able to look at the world and laugh at its ridiculous ways, being able to cling to their beliefs, because of the certainty they had in their own convictions.

Even more, they would have to be a person of deep love, unafraid of sharing that love with those all around them. Love is the very core of life, Not unlike the molten lava at the earth's center, the fire that keeps our earth together and in perfect balance.

So if you're not old and lost like me, uncertain of your direction and more unsure of your destination, use that wonderful energy that only the young possess, and find your way while you have the time and can. Don't let your life slip away, leaving you unfulfilled, empty and alone.

Michael Becker

Words

Words are the gentlest way to caress and stimulate
the most creative of minds.
Drawing or painting a thing of beauty,
using words as the brush,
the mind as the canvas, is so grand,
As grand as a river rushing to the sea
through a rocky crevice,
past boulders trying to block or impede,
its never ending journey.
Words flowing off the end of one's tongue
can remove the boulders.
Smoothing out the canyon walls,
walls of life, giving inner peace.
Words can make the warm love
that flows through one's soul boil,
turning it to a raging river of passion,
that nothing on this earth can stop.
Words can also turn you cold as ice,
Making you appear as if you were made of stone.
Choose your words carefully.
Trying never to offend,
Words are valuable
and should only be used in the very best intent
anything else would be a waste.

Walking Tall

As I search down into people's hearts,
and pocketbook, for a dollar or two,
a special person comes to mind.
On January the seventeenth nineteen-ninety-eight,
Mike Becker will step up to the bowling lane,
and attempt to throw the first ball, for Muscular Dystrophy.
Let me tell you about my friend.
He has taught me to listen to all the wonderful sounds,
To smell all the beautiful flowers,
and listen to the rain, as it freshens our earth.
He was our Chief of Police,
when this horrible muscle disease tried to knock him down;
what a loss to our community,
for he was always there to help the young and old.
Our teenagers, he saved from going down the wrong road.
Through open heart surgery, and diabetes,
he has beaten the odds, he is still walking tall.
So go ahead, Mike, and throw that ball.
For when you do, we will all walk with you,
to conquer this disease.
Walk tall my friend,
We are with you.

Written by my friend Jan
At the Muscular Dystrophy Kickoff

Michael Becker

10TH PRECINCT

LIGHT SHADOWS

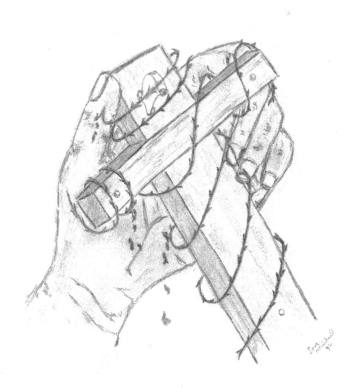

PRAIRIE DOG

michael 90

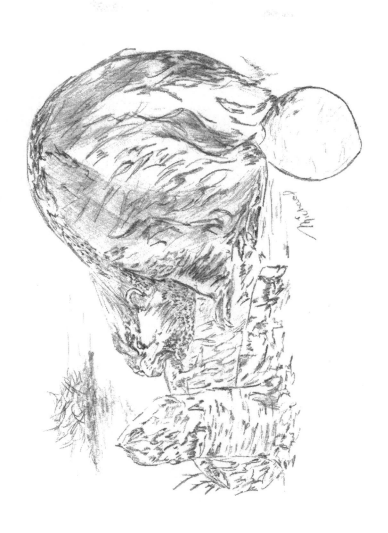

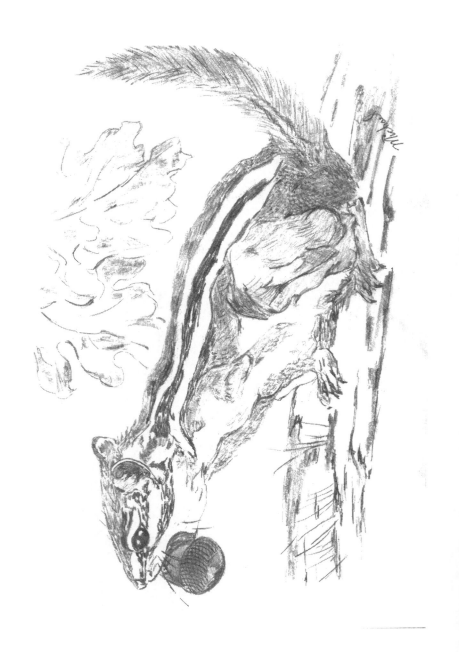

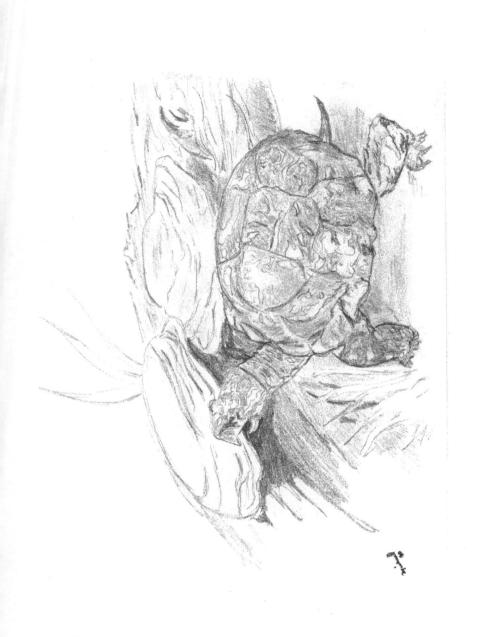

64544813R00110

Made in the USA
Lexington, KY
12 June 2017